American Manscape

American Manscape

by Daniel Romo

~ 2026 ~

American Manscape

Cover art
Daniel Romo

Book design
Michael Wada

Moon Tide logo design
Abraham Gomez

American Manscape
is published by Moon Tide Press

Moon Tide Press
6709 Washington Ave. #9297
Whittier, CA 90608
www.moontidepress.com

FIRST EDITION

Printed in the United States of America

ISBN # 978-1-957799-54-4

Contents

Foreword

These days masculinity looks a lot less like Clint Eastwood riding into an American sunset and more like a gym bro in Costco eyeballing a wall of collagen tubs, wondering if "marine-based" means he's microdosing the dust of a decommissioned submarine. It's a sleepless guy streaming a YouTube video called "How to Be More Present Every Single Moment" at 1.75x speed while checking fantasy football scores, juggling wild prop bets, and trying to convince himself this casino of laptop tabs still counts as self-improvement. Or it's a single dad in a lawn chair at his daughter's soccer game, refreshing his app feed like it's a scoreboard, pretending to watch the match while wondering if he's been shadow banned or if the whole world muted him because he's just not putting up numbers anymore. The literary man, we're told by endless think pieces, is dead. Long live the literary man. American masculinity writ large is in crisis, but it isn't at a crossroads so much as it has taken to the backroads. It's obscene, offscreen.

That's the strange terrain *American Manscape* wanders through: the everyman in all his confused, tender, and often absurd splendor. Daniel Romo's poems don't offer us updated versions of the old myths; instead, they deliver poignant dispatches from the newfangled now, where the speakers are half awake, half hopeful, fully online, and still capable of surprising themselves with small moments of wonder amid all this American noise.

In "Dad Jokes," Romo weaponizes this much-maligned form of comedy to talk about divorce, regret, and the way memory refuses to stay in its lane: "most of our lives have already delivered so / many punchlines," the speaker says, and the rest of the piece goes about proving that thesis. We get an image of the Hulk at a kid's birthday party, but this Hulk is "a balding man…in a shoddy costume," a guy whose own life looks like it's survived a smash or two. The speaker understands that "comedy is all about timing," and the kicker here is that the timing's off: the joke lands late—after the divorce, after the party, after the kid has blown out the candles and gone to bed. In the end, the poem suggests a very American verity: a lot of our "heroes" are just deflated guys in bad suits, struggling to stay in character.

If "Dad Jokes" hangs out at the kids' party, "Second Marriage" lives in the kitchen and the laundry room, where the honeymoon has been replaced by chores. Here, the speaker questions the idea of sequels—"usually worse / than the original"—and gold stars ("why is gold the standard when silver's so / much prettier?"). From there the poem becomes a kind of anti-self-help guide. It pushes back against the idea of optimization, specifically Malcolm Gladwell's 10,000-hour rule, and wonders how many hours it takes to be "just okay at something / you need simply to get by," whether you can just "fake it until they break it." When Rocky appears at the end of the piece, having learned "how to do his own laundry, / how to separate the light from the dark," it's hilarious, yes, but it's also a clear redefinition of victory. In Romo's book, the champion is not a boxer with his arms raised atop the stone steps outside the entrance to the Philadelphia Museum of Art. It's the man sorting socks alone at midnight, still trying.

If "Dad Jokes" and "Second Marriage" stay close to the family, "On 8th and Pine" walks the block. The poem opens with two men who "can't throw a punch," a fight that never quite erupts, and compares a "gust of wild haymakers" to "a multitude of prayers / from those who've never bowed / their heads." Even here, where we expect blood and bravado, Romo undercuts the usual script. The skater is locked into "a life of shuv-its and kickflips," the grinds between board and bench forming a "holy / union," and the speaker stands in the middle of it all and says, "I'm most me when / my surroundings resemble all that / I'm not." Manhood in this poem isn't about being the toughest guy on the corner. It's about being the one who can read the street, who can see that "slice / of life divided into segments so clear" that the way you choose to step out of the scene, "how you end the poem," is "how you begin the rest / of your life."

What I love most about this book, Romo's sixth poetry collection, is how unheroic its heroics are. These aren't brazen characters climbing impossible mountains or cliff diving in Acapulco. They're just regular guys trying to survive group text threads, tedious commutes, and losing seasons with their dignity intact. In "Produce," a colonoscopy becomes a meditation on the surveillance state. In "Playing 90's R&B on my Way to Work While Driving Down PCH," a commute becomes a rolling nostalgia trip as the speaker belts along with old love songs while weaving through traffic, surrounded by "a multi-genre mixed tape / with no sense of clarity / and cohesion." These are poems for anyone who's ever looked up from the soft light of their phone in the middle of the night and wondered: Is this it? And: Is this enough?

In *American Manscape*, the answers aren't intrepid or cinematic, but beautifully human: yes, duh. Because we're still here, trying and failing, still finding joy in the strangeness of a guy holding a Free Hugs sign in a supermarket parking lot or the inherent poetry of a fresh cup of coffee or finding oneself stuck in a traffic jam behind a parade of rowdy bikers. The literary man is dead. Long live the literary man.

— Ryan Ridge, author of *New Bad News*

We are each of us—every single one of us—
meant to be a lens for truths that we ourselves cannot see.

—Christian Wiman

Look, I'm still in America (yeah)
Beautiful, elegant, sinful, and arrogant (woo).

—Lecrae

Second Marriage

Everyone knows sequels are usually worse
than the original and second-guessing isn't

preferable to simply going with your gut.
I'm all for stars being stuck to the top of

the page noting a child's best efforts, but
why is gold the standard when silver's so

much prettier? I have loved and lost and
learned that beating oneself up only ends

in a draw. Gladwell says to become an
expert at something it takes 10,000 hours

of practice, but I wonder how many hours
it takes to become just okay at something

you need simply to get by and if one can
just fake it until they break it. I'm still

learning the value of domesticity—how to
maximize dishwasher space and when to

confess to my wife that my soul feels like
it's been forgotten in the dryer and keeps

tumbling with each new load. Rocky loses
in the first film but wins in the next because

I imagine he vowed he and Adrian will never
throw in the towel and in the process he's

learned how to how do his own laundry,
how to separate the light from the dark,

the pains from the stains.

2nd Street Baptismal

For the Long Beach Rippers

It's the same as when clouds refuse to behave
the way they're drawn and the front half lifts,
points, and floats a little more towards Heaven.
And the back half can't be mad because what
body wouldn't want to stretch itself to weave
its way in and out of stars yet to be navigated
and named? That's my point of view when the
bicycle pack highjacks the boulevard and riders
laugh and wear motorists' honks like badges
doubling as bandages for impending falls.
And though they swerve down the street in
between raucous and reckless, I imagine how
proud their parents would be watching them
wheelie all the way from one part of town to
the other. Because there's inherent beauty to
one being so careless yet careful at the same
time. To be so young and bold as to zigzag
amongst oncoming cars like they're stationary
cones requires a sensitivity and stamina
enhanced by the soundtrack of each spinning
wheel. Traffic is forced to follow as if trailing
a parade not longed to be a part of, but who
can argue with this type of takeover when
children stare from backseats of their parents'
cars and what they witness contradicts
everything they've been told about wearing
a helmet. We savor moments like this because
we know our bodies won't always be able to
travel the direction we want them to be steered,
and the day will come when both tires must
stay firmly on earth and we peddle a more
sensible line, remembering how we offered
our hearts to the pavement and our front
wheels to God.

Forecast

I'm transfixed on the window on this rare
Southern California rainy day, imagining

the drops are glad to finally get their own
feet wet, even if the terrain is all lack of

traction and oil slick, pondering how one
would give back borrowed time because

there's something so contemplative about
the duo of gray sky and undeserved grace.

I just read about a Japanese man who hasn't
spoken to his wife in 30 years, and don't

shoot the translator, but communicating
for decades via nothing but nods and grunts

is a love language so basic and primal, it
should be regarded as the beginning of

intimacy. But the iciness between skin and
the coldest of shoulders creates a frostbite

so damaging, sometimes the only way to
heal is to sever the limbs, despite years after

the dissolution of arm and torso, best and
friend, man and wife, the body still can feel

the sensations that tap like the nervousness
of aborted toes long after the amputation.

So we do the best we can—slow down, avoid
haphazard lane changes, and wait for the light

and warmth of the sun, all while navigating life
through conditions we never learned to drive in.

Blading

The politician wasn't struck in the assassination attempt
and only his ear was grazed, but the trickle of his blood caused
        half the country to cry, *Hero!*
        and the other half to yell, *Staged!*
though no one can deny
octogenarians are more brittle bones
than bulletproof, and
all's fair in love and reward.

There are those who claim we never landed on the Moon
and those who maintain the Earth is flat,
yet that doesn't change the fact that
        Abdullah the Butcher
secretly sliced his forehead with a razorblade during matches
in the days when wrestling was supposed to be
                considered real,
and his blood poured down onto his opponents
like a christening for non-believers in the crowd
at a baptism rooted in amusement
and self-mutilation.

My dad didn't initially recognize me as I visited
him and my mom this weekend
and blamed it on his cataracts.
And while that may be the cause,
I clearly see what's to come
for us all.

            When a platform is based upon pretending
            and failure to acknowledge that it's not true sport
            but entertainment,
            who could blame the public's skepticism
            when a former president is clipped by a sniper
            and seconds later raises his fist to Heaven
            as if not giving praise, but
            milking the most out of Life's misses.

I'm sure the candidate will still be able to hear
from his right ear
but never listen.

I'm sure my dad will continue to deny
the natural byproducts of his age

because lies build like
scar tissue piled up upon skin,
like fresh dirt piled upon
graves.

Imposter Syndrome

I'm not feeling like myself today, but the forecast
calls for faking it until I make it, and I wonder if
the horizon ever wants to phone it in by cloning
the day before because it also feels like a knockoff.
Last year's Superbowl winner is the odds-on favorite
again, and is it wrong I find it so easy to root against
perennials and pull for the weeds? I recently told
my wife I hadn't changed a tire in twenty years and
confess I don't know if I still could but assume it's
like riding a bike, yet what happens if it's a unicycle
with a flat of its own? This is the summer Maui's
on fire and much of the country experiences record
highs and call this coincidence or Mother Nature's
way of saying, *I've been trying to tell you meteorological*
numbers don't lie to those who deny global warming.
It takes a village to cultivate the land and the wave
of coordinated L.A. mall robberies show even
Southern California and the Pacific Ocean don't
always provide enough water and sunlight, but
lack of upbringing and morals isn't regional
because the former president and his circle now
being indicted is just another form of a flash mob
smash and grab. Sometimes we belong and other
times we truly don't and to recognize the difference
is to possess the wherewithal to declare a state of
emergency or doubt while residing on an island all
your own, holding a fruity, tropical drink in one
hand, waving a flaming white flag with the other.

Maritime

I told my wife the luxury Cybertruck we passed on the
405 South is bulletproof, and she found her Bible she

thought was lost under my passenger seat when we
arrived home, and somewhere between departure and

arrival, she laughed and asked, *What is this world coming
to?* But I didn't answer because how does one respond

when the trinity of traffic, impenetrability, and book
of Revelations are concerned? They're discontinuing

my sweetener at the coffee shop and I appreciate that
I was given a personalized heads-up, but it sucks when

you know you will no longer be able to savor a flavor
in which amidst life's various seasons you both swam

laps and drowned in. There are libraries where people
are loaned to readers to share their stories and my

autobiography might be titled *Flailing at Midnight in an
Ocean of Green Tea with Anklefuls of Heavy Seaweed but*

*Mustering the Will to Doggie Paddle Back to an Open-armed
Shore.* So often, when it seems our limbs are shattered

oars and we are left to float sans current or hope, a
mystery tide guides us back to familiar land, and we

can choose to look back at it as plunge or purification.
If someone were to search for me, they could most

likely find me somewhere between belief and the self-
help section. And after they checked me out and I

narrated, they might marvel as I paused my story mid-
sentence to pull yet another piece of kelp from my

mouth that acts a permanent bookmark reminding
me never to lose my place or faith.

Acupressure

My skin has never been this intimate
with another man's hands
was my foremost thought as the masseuse
oiled and lacquered my limbs,
mining hurt my body hasn't learned
to release.

I know the mechanics of hoarding pain
the way I comprehend how muscle memory
allows for both
hedonism and healing,
but him burrowing into me was a lesson
in what I never knew
ached the most.

We're told to dig deeper when we
appear to have nothing left to give
and that's the price we pay for
our faulty stamina and generosity.

It is possible to be both a giver and a taker,
a wick, flame, and a candlestick maker.

On the surface
I'm a canvas of flesh stretched out amongst
memories and a muscular physique.
But underneath,

I'm just a man lying face down in a dark room
naming each wince,
marveling how fingers can produce
vowels that still singe long after
the last touch.

Last Night Just Before Midnight I Ordered Calvin Klein Boxer Briefs on eBay

Because I now fit the demographic where the fabric
on my body is more important than where I bought

it from, and learning to be comfortable in my own
skin is an auction in itself in which I've finally learned

to become the highest bidder. Ever marvel at how
easy it is to buy your way into a life that's so convenient

but forget the cost it took to achieve one-day shipping?
My pastor is also a drummer and in his sermon said

when his sticks flub a beat, he just calls it jazz, and
on these late nights when I'm so awake that I debate

purchasing new underwear or Tupperware lids, I can
sometimes still feel the pulse of improvisation for

which I've composed my share of records. There are
people that make a living buying and selling and there

are those who spend their lives seeking out bargains,
and that symbiotic musicality is like a concert where

both headliner and audience live off the lyrics and
limelight. And then there are those who remain stuck

in their solos, tapping their foot on the mattress under
the darkness of covers as if keeping time to each past

mistake, just looking for their chance at an encore.

Forget-me-nots

Living in someone's shadow is a part of domesticity not to be confused with making your own bed and lying in it. One is a matter of feeling clean and snug under the comforter. The other is a matter of no one taking note of the subtleties in your crown molding. Feeling like a houseguest under the weight your own doormat is the literal Southernmost form of hospitality, and no amount of homemade mac and cheese can ease feelings of inadequacy. Because being overlooked is a hurt akin to being lost, and finding your way requires backtracking rooted in clearing bramble that still bears pieces of your flesh posing as flowers. Though who mentions the romanticism in leaving fertile parts of yourself in unassuming gardens? I walked through the Botanical Body Parts and pricked my finger on a thorn that I recognized as pieces of my fingernail. I know from experience, if you've ever been offered a bouquet comprised of a species that you can't quite name, recall the bloom… absorb the scent… become the wilting.

Leap Year

Most people don't know that addressing
the elephant in the room with any degree

of civility has been added to the list of
endangered species. Or that chivalry is

deadpan, not deceased. Or how to write
a cursive capital Q. I was elated to learn

that *Toxic Toast Records* is an actual place
because the best businesses double as

both name and way of life, and few things
are better than absorbing the crackle of

vintage vinyl while repping outlaw breakfast
staples. In the 80s, kids under a hundred

pounds ate free at *The Big Yellow House*
and today an abundance of children

from that decade who wore adult sizes
in third grade teach Saturday spin classes

at the Y. What doesn't break us, shapes
us, and the Toughskin jeans we wore

have contoured our Gen X bodies as if
helping us size up the trauma. I appreciate

the idea of trigger warnings, but are those
notices not both spoiler and stifling natural

order? Last year my birthday fell on a
Sunday and this year it was on a Tuesday,

and it's amazing how the days can leap
and sneak up from one year into the next

as if hiding in waiting behind tall grass
on the savannas as silently waiting to

poach our psyche.

Dad Jokes

I won't ask you what the salad dressing said to
the lettuce or what you call a podiatrist allergic

to toes because most of our lives have already
delivered so many punchlines with so little guts

left to stomach the pain. Yesterday I went to a
kid's birthday party and was reminded how my

ex-wife and I paid quite the sum for The Hulk
to entertain at our son's party where a balding

man showed up in a shotty costume as if all his
muscles and might had been deflated by a divorce

of his own. It's a funny thing these memories
that almost possess you like superpowers, not

ha-ha funny, but more so nervous-laughter
funny, as if that's the only response you could

make while paying your last respects to a person,
place, or marriage you never really knew. I

appreciate that comedy is all about timing, and
I can now see the days when I replied, *Who's there?*

were both question and response to myself as
if trying to see what I was willing to let go of

and what I was willing to let in. I'll spare you
the one about the father and time because that's

a cruel one in which you can't tell the wounds
that have healed from the ones that remain a riddle.

Blowing Out Candles

For Devan

My adult son is moving away,
and though we've been living in
different households for years,
this soon-to-be distance between
California and New York is both
        a state of geography and condition—
            like Duluth and disbelief,
            Sheboygan and shock,
            Denver and denial
where my prayer is a one-way ticket to Heaven
that we're able to navigate our relationship
across a past of trying times
  and time zones.

And in the process of him packing,
my hope is that he can recall
how I was the youngest parent
and only dad
at classmates' Saturday birthday parties
            amongst a P.T.A. of mothers
who knew which teachers you wanted
your child to have next year
because they had done this all
before.

And maybe if he unearths any construction books
he might still possess from toddlerhood,
he can forgive me for any debris remaining
from any foundations
                        I failed to build.

What is the term for being able to simultaneously
move forward and away
while mending?

At what point does a memory become
bulldozed?

My son,
thrive in your new life
three hours ahead of me and
light years passed me
as a man,
and father.
And if you ever dream under the Brooklyn skyline
of how you used to fall asleep in the backseat of my car,
your head fallen to the side,
comatose from too much candy and cake,
just know I will always be here
to help pick it back up.

House Specials

The restaurant my former student owns just earned a Michelin
star is something I never imagined would come up in

conversation. Why would I ever picture a nondescript
man ordering a sampling of her menu to dissect what

separates them from the steakhouse across town? Still,
I wondered how he'd rate me if he blended in the back

of my English class during third period in a hoodie and
jeans and abruptly left just as I explained the importance

of logical fallacies. Because who judges us and the extent
to which we'll go to please people varies from clique to

clique and we often grade our best and worst moments
on a curve with an unattainable rubric set for ourselves.

In a therapy session to learn how to better connect with
my wife, I felt the harshness of my words and both the

food critic and myself might highjack the vernacular of
my students to confess, *Damn. That's mid,* conveying our

deflated feelings regarding my direct methods of
communication. I explain to my in-laws over a plate

of safe and neat Pad Thai that I prefer eating at a place
that isn't so sterilized, where the silverware is spotted

and decade-old wads of gum are balled up under each
table because there is nothing more authentic than

recognizing the need for improvement while presenting
yourself as you are—the orange letters in *Mongkut's Thai*

House emblazoned on top of the building, the T dangling
to the right like a crooked apology.

Green Thumb

I'd argue some plants prefer gray sky
over sunlight. And some clouds long

to dissipate, à la kamikaze ice crystals.
And just because you claim to have

the magic touch doesn't mean you
can pull a rabbit from your hatchback.

Sometimes seeing is bereaving, and
pulling the wool over someone's eyes

or fleecing them begs to ask why the
sheep became a symbol of deception

when it stands for sacrifice in the Bible.
I understand natural selection, but I'm

lost when it comes to how long leftovers
can survive in the fridge and why dogs

are no longer named Fido. I marvel at
the way growth occurs with drops that

aren't distributed to scale and at those
who can keep anything alive during

personal droughts as if horticulture
chooses the resiliency of roots. And

when I'm absorbing too much darkness
and dehydration, I whisper, *Abracadabra,*

as if any second a bunny will spring out
from a Civic.

Happy Hour

When I want to introduce my
oldest childhood friend to someone,
my impulse is to say,
We were the best men in each other's
            first weddings,
but I hold off because I wonder if that's
a testament to our decades-long friendship
or revelation of shared
                  failures,
and when the new barista overflowed the pitcher
with scolding water and blamed it on
technical difficulties,
I ask if that's deflection using humor or
lack of accountability.

When the degree to which our mistakes reach
the boiling point and we are finally able to
stick our hands inside the pot we stirred
to sift out the silt and guilt
from the pits of our past,
we are finally ready to savor and appreciate
the refill.

I've often heard people say someone did a
360 in their life when they meant a 180,
but coming full circle sounds like
so much more of an achievement,
and when my oldest childhood friend helped me
with my tie at the alter,
securing a knot that would ultimately
undo for
both of us,
maybe that wasn't an oversight in binding
but a lesson in handling
                    the unraveling.

The coffee shop soundtrack plays
cover songs of 80's hits,
and I sip my tea listening intently to
each familiar melody
as if the past is the
honeymoon period
and today all drinks
are half off for
newlyweds.

Playing 90's R&B on My Way to Work While Driving Down PCH

I sing along as if all the begging
to win the girl back would also cut
the traffic in half and I understand how
    a quartet is the ideal number for
    harmonizing in
    seeking forgiveness.

I wish I could say this gray morning is a lonely road,
but it's burgeoning with commuters
weaving in and out of lanes like
a multi-genre mixed tape
with no sense of clarity
and cohesion.

The crooners confess they weren't perfect,
and we should all be so lucky as to
be able to belt out soulful
apologies that ring falsetto but
sing more like façade,
such as City View Terrace and
Vista Gardens Apartments,
        more languish
than lush—
though off-key shower voices ring
with even more honesty.

And even if the lyrics were more feel-good
than follow-through,
sometimes we need to hear passionate pleas
from velvet-suited men on bended knee
just to get us through the day,
or decade.

I reach my destination yet
they beseech me to come back
because they swear to change their ways,
and isn't that how it is when

we move on but forget the route we took
to get there,
as if the years passed by and left us behind,
forced to replay the soundtracks of every
trying commute
we've ever taken.

Empty Nest

What's the term for when a dad's home alone,
sitting in the corner of his living room left

holding his feelings and fate, cradled in his
arms like a fresh bouquet of carnations and

consolations? And what's it called when you
have *too* much time to stop and smell the newly

bloomed juxtaposes? There is nothing new
under the pun or words to define when a man

becomes a syndrome—but most folks don't
know the Burrowing Owl has evolved to dwell

comfortably in abandoned dens to escape the
heat, and the barista and customer each ask

how their days are, both responding, *not the best
or worst* because it turns out, both still live with

their exes, going to show getting out of the
kitchen isn't solely a matter of temperature,

but temperament. Birds learn from each other
and mimic the most successful ways to build

and humans copy one another by replicating
the most effective ways to fall apart, but what

of the father rocking back and forth in his favorite
recliner, flapping his arms as if hoping to take off

and fly backwards into second chances and
flew-by seasons.

Passengers

My wife confessed she closes her eyes on
the scarier rides and I'm unsure if I feel
relief that she sleeps on her fears
or betrayed because I have a bird's-eye view
from heights I thought we'd face
together as stated
                    in our vows.
She's a talker and I'm a silenter—
        the clankety-clank of the coaster going
        up… up… up…
and the tongue-tied pause just before
the descent.

The old barista asks the new barista,
What better way to learn than to jump in?
and I concur to cannonball is more effective
than to tiptoe
and an incorrectly made drink amongst
small talk with customers beats
being isolated in the breakroom watching
training videos.

We said we'd challenge ourselves each visit
by going on something that scares us
and while a roller coaster is the layman's
life metaphor,
last week my daughter and I listened to a
cover band playing in the park and
I'd argue that a career of performing
someone else's songs
is an even more apt comparison
because she says,
            At least they still have dreams,
and not giving up while impersonating
someone else is the ultimate test of
being secure in your own long hair
and leopard-skin pants.

Next time, I'll tell my wife we'll raise our arms
during the drop in solidarity
as if celebrating the first leg of a tour
we take turns headlining,
        the lead singer who belts out vocals like
        conquered nightmares,
        and the tight-lipped drummer
        tapping his foot
        like etching moments
        into time.

Season Passholder

I took a survey from the amusement park just to tell
them their nachos suck, and I hope my feedback will

help them see boasting the West Coast's tallest tower
of terror isn't grounds for skimping on authenticity

and fresh ingredients. I struggle with when to tell the
truth and when to find ways to step around it as if

my words are potholes no public works department
has been able to fill in which so many tires have

thudded down without warning, and isn't that how
we feel when the punches to our guts are actually

love taps designed not to knock out our wind, but
to simply knock in some sense? The job awaiting me

is a perfect fit, but is to go from daily breathing in a
Long Beach ocean breeze to struggling to exist in an

Austin summertime sauna grounds for questioning
the doors that are opened for me versus the cracked

windows someone forgot to close? Then again, maybe
it is okay to brag about the heights you possess because

allowing a man to survey his life from two hundred
feet before he falls to the earth is an attraction that

can't be taken for granted because who doesn't want
a view of their life, unobstructed, blazoned with clarity,

ripe with flavor.

August

Today is Wednesday,
midweek when the marina
hosts my favorite farmer's market.
   Some refer to today as *hump*,
but when is getting over on yourself
something you should aim for?

The patrons stroll from stand to stand,
holding up cartons of produce to their faces,
speculating how it will taste
                                                  and age.

I'm unsure how to feel about turning
50 next month,
but the mirror reflecting
a muscular frame demonstrating
all the weight it's learned to carry
as if it couldn't let me in on
the necessity of
                    no pain… no gain
            is rooting for embrace.

The cover band croons,
my wife and I eat homemade pupusas,
and the coral evening sky
begs to be eulogized before
another
workday.

I reflect on my mortality more so than ever
and ponder the anatomy of a legacy,
the way it weaves in and out of
loved ones' lives like the ripeness of
yesteryear,
the freshness
of tomorrow.

Lines that Stuck Out After Watching *The Notebook* for the First Time at 49 or Things I say to Myself 6 Months from When I Turn 50?

If you're a bird, I'm a bird.
    I'm not a carpenter.
    But I'm an expert craftsman at building up
    sky-high expectations:
        flailing, wishful,
    unfulfilled.

I want all of you, forever, everyday.
You and me... everyday.
    We thought we'd have accomplished more
    by now—I whisper to myself in plural.

It was an improbable romance.
He was a country boy.
She was from the city.
    The capitol and name of my current state
    are both named "Loss."

There are no monuments dedicated to me
and my name will soon be forgotten.
    I wonder if my wife was truly able to hear the echoes in
    the caverns of my void when I told her
    I understand why men my age undergo mid-life crises.

This is my home now.
    A door opens. Two close.
    Where are all the houses that are
    on the market?

You are and always have been, my dream.
    If I close my eyes tight enough, I feel the
    breeze from the latest decade of my life
    passing me by as if salute followed by
    sendoff.

It was real, wasn't it? You and me.
Such a long time ago, we were just a couple of kids.
But we really loved each other, didn't we?
Why did it take me so many years to realize
we are not the men we used to be?

I just pray that I mattered.
Science goes only so far and then comes God.

June Gloom

I appreciate the ambiguity and wet blanketness of a wishy-washy sky. Is breaking free from darkness an achievement to be celebrated if there was already so much sun and certainty? Not many scholars know the honorary degree birthed the asterisk. After the man in front of the grocery store holding a sign that read "Free Hugs" was embraced by the woman who said, *Sometimes I just wanna be gone from this world,* he reminded and chided her, *Ma'am, you possess a Ph.D. in worth.* The forecast can only call for tropical storms named after the worst version of yourself when weather dictates moods. Clouds are never an inconvenience but to be celebrated as if a mixture of recovering and moving on from trauma for the world to behold before they dissipate, leaving room for interpretation that allows for so many lost heads and poor men's justification for self-pity.

New Reign

Technology now allows us to pay with our palms
and scanning body parts is the new express lane,

though this advancement hasn't progressed to
reading the irony of this convenience in relation

to degree of buyer calluses. So much can be
said for earning an honest day's wage and the

new president says he's gonna impose 10,000%
tariffs because he claims other countries owe us

for all we've done for them, and the line between
patriotism and pridefulness has always been drawn

by bloody hands and congress. The middle-aged
man playing an online game beside me at my

favorite coffee shop grunts as his kingdom gets
captured, so I can't help but peer over and wince

when he's down to an army of archers and a harpist
because the joke's on us when we fancy ourselves

emperor but are more court jester. If during our
most introspective moments, we survey the land

and see the cost of the legacy or loss we've created,
we can decipher how much each casualty amounts

to. Instead, we swipe our hands and take our groceries
so we can plop down into our La-Z-Boys to stab

our scepters into the earth as if staking our claim
to this cold, new world.

Proclamation

The baristas don't allow homeless people to
use the restrooms at this coffee shop because

they leave a mess behind, and I struggle with
the notion of protocol vs. person, when to

enforce the offensiveness of the scent and
when to divorce the stench from the descent.

And in the movie I watched last night, the
widower told the pop star that having an

image isn't having a life and I wondered if
that should be printed in a flourishing font

towards the bottom of the coffee cup for
all customers to read just before they toss

them in the trash. I'm at a point in my life
where I want what's just to reign down like

a steady precipitation in which everyone
desires to open their mouths to replace

the sixty percent of their body that is water
with a fresh flood of humanity and new

perspective. The employees give the bathroom
code to those who pay for their goods and I

only order a drink here because I feel obligated
since I spend so much time using their Wi-Fi.

But my guilt doesn't prevent me from walking
out the door and yelling, *1-3-4-6-8!* as if letting
the world know all are welcome.

Election

A straw poll was taken and the leading candidate is *Getting lost in someone else's dreams.* A surprising, distant second was *Taking out the trash barefoot in a Midwest snowstorm.* It seems frostbite complements of a frozen Fargo tundra isn't the challenger one might think. Something about living out someone else's aspirations deeply resonated within the voters. When asked why she selected that, a middle-aged, single woman who directs Hallmark movies said, *I couldn't stand the guilt I'd feel knowing this fantasy isn't mine.* An octogenarian who enjoys days of Dominoes and Bonanza marathons confided, *It's just not right. Not everyone imagines tending to the Ponderosa alongside Little Joe and Hoss.* I understand the dynamics of being stuck in a world rooted in a make-believe where the fiction is written without the protagonist in mind. Still, I wonder why no one voted for *Rock-bottom blues familiarity,* recalling the snapping of fingers, bobbing heads up and down, a gutting twang demanding to be worst nightmare and running mate.

Taking Roll

On my way home from teaching Saturday school,
Latino preachers chant on the corner of
PCH and Long Beach Boulevard
            that hell awaits the eternity
for those who haven't repented.
I don't know the Spanish translation of *couth*
and I'm certain they're unsure of its meaning
in any language
because I feel like the words
blaring from the megaphones
will turn these inner-city streets beneath me
to brimstone   at any moment.

The students have been absent too much
so this is their punishment,
and maybe our school would benefit from
teachers standing in front of the campus
screaming,
            "Come to class or you'll be a failure… forever!"

We could all use some form of intervention,
some type of personal plea showing us that
our current course on *Failure to be Present Lane*
                        and *Unfaithfulness Ave.*
can still be corrected.

But the difference between convicting
and convincing
is the difference in a major assignment with
a final grade scrawled
on the top of the page
or a personal note in the margin informing of
the way and opportunity
                for a redo.

Sometimes scare tactics are the poor man's gentleness,
and the effectiveness of each can be measured by
the look on the faces of the parishioners
          sitting in the front row.

I'll return next week
as will the students,
earning time served for simply saying,
Here, as if it's always
that easy to earn life credit for
                    everything.

From *1915 Rules for Teachers*

Found Poem

1. You will not marry in ice cream stores.

2. You are not to keep company with
   men who dress in bright colors
   between the hours of 8 p.m. and 6 a.m.

3. You must be home to smoke cigarettes and
   start the fire.

4. You may not loiter with your father or brother
   or carriage or automobile.

5. You may not travel with dye in your hair.

6. You may not ride the blackboards
   unless attending a school function.

7. You may not scrub the chairman of the board.

8. You may not warm hot water.

9. You may under no circumstances teach men
   to wear petticoats above the ankle.

10. You must contract clean men.

11. Your dresses must wear dresses.

12. To keep the school room neat,
    you must have permission
    to sweep the city.

Pamplona

I paid the Piper in pocket change and pimento loaf. One form of currency for my debt and the other to satisfy a distinct hunger I'm certain he doesn't know he longs for. An assortment of meats and other ingredients is an acquired taste and I have yet to leap off the cliffs of Acapulco into the Pacific, but I might love it and be a natural for all I know. We rarely stop to consider combinations that don't seem to complement each other like devil and eggs, like snails and facials, like top-tier vacation packages and running from bulls. And in in that way, we never give ourselves the opportunity to experience our utmost exfoliation or the rush of fleeing from beasts we never imagined we'd be able to outrun. The Piper will thank me for being a stand-up guy as he needs those quarters for the lone pay phone when he's lost along a stretch of remote highway and for eating such a misunderstood food. And I'll thank him when I strip off all my clothes, squeeze into a speedo, and soar from a Mexican precipice wondering where this glorious wind has been all my life and crash down into an ocean that welcomes me as if I'd just broken the plane between day and dream.

Half Day

Nothing to do with existence is a passive act.
Seize the day not *Let the calendar adhere to its own*

intervals. Even if all I do is eat pretzels while
staring out the window on this Thursday

morning at the café, just being here is a
luxury; all the action in front of me on the

avenue—them moments is designer duds.
I watched a woman attempt to fit a big-ass

dresser into her tiny-bottom hatchback and
was torn between wanting to help and warn

since the struggle to fit something into a
space that doesn't seem to welcome it is

its own form of natural order, and the fact
my brother-in-law reduced his consumption

of red meat but refuses to wear a helmet
while biking through busy streets is a

commentary on trusting others more so
than yourself. Granted was not made to

be taken, although stolen moments should
be celebrated and seized for rainy days

when happiness decides to call in sick
and all that's left is the lingering saltiness

of a comfort snack, the remnants of flavor
from a filet mignon, the time it takes to

count your blessings and burials.

Spam

Hi Daniel. I am Viktoriya. the skywatcher and fixer.
Your handle grabbed my eye, and I'd adore to discuss
stellar mysteries and fascinating talks. Down?

— from my email spam folder

Sometimes we shoot for the stars just to feel lauded
for landing on some version of the moon. The crushing

feeling of coming back to earth is foreign territory in
a space that lacks gravity. So when the employee asks

his new co-worker if she likes to party and she replies
about moderation, I know it's her way of informing

him to please be quiet and keep making other people's
sandwiches. I haven't spoken to my brother in years

because of something he said, and though I've forgiven
him, like the unused mystery key on my keychain, I still

don't know where he fits into my life. I have learned
the science of doors and the exaggerated squeaks in

movies is a manufactured sound signaling a warning
only the audience is privy to. And if you arrive late

because the concession stand was so crowded, the
protagonist might stare at the camera to say, *You're*

own your own. The couple that met while placing first
and second in a taco eating contest spent the rest of

their lives competing to see who could consume each
meal first and understands the importance of slowing

down to savor the decadence and deliberateness of
dessert. And even though it's her first day, the new

employee is right. Because even constellations know
when to shine bright and when to glow just faint

enough to be seen, as if saving themselves for nights
when we look up to be reminded that discovery starts

with ourselves.

Diss Track

The origin of a hip-hop beef is seasoned
with special sauce and
          Slauson's finest hype men.

A feud rooted in accusations of
appropriation is a (rap) battle for the ages,
authenticity, and
audience approval.

Wop, wop, wop,
          wop, wop!

It becomes personal when a man's
motives, morals, and music
are called into question
all in one.

Calling out and crip-walking all over
one's (stage) name is no doubt
a slander to be handled
because being hard
protects a soft ego.

          Hoodlife my ass more like phony contrive /
          Street cred, psh, boy you rep Rodeo Drive.

It's a fickle world, this rap game—
where artists go from
collaborators to haters,

  from OG to enemy,

    from riding
      to dying.

Revision

Let's say we're seahorses. Let's say our forgotten birthday candles
have melted into coral. Let's say the coral is forgotten, too.
Let's say the water is repetition. It is high tide. We have washed ashore.
The children scoop us up with plastic shovels.
They drop us into half-filled buckets of sandy water
hoping to revive us.
Their mothers convince them to throw us back.
Our bodies turn to foam.
We are already dead.

Let's say we're notorious bank robbers planning our heist from
our hideout.
Let's say our masks are big yellow happy faces.
Let's say we are bad men.
Our mothers have written us letters trying to convince us
to turn ourselves in.
We rip them up and smile. We were always disobedient children.
Let's say we're cops who have been tipped off,
about to raid the hideout.
Let's say our guns are loaded, and our laughs are loud.

Let's say we're liars and none of this happened.
Let's say we were seahorses.
Let's say our birthdays were never celebrated.
Let's say we've crossed out those times in our lives.

Let's say we're convenient
rough drafts.

Variables

Your Algebra is lovely.
By lovely I mean, I scoop your entrails out with a plastic fork
and swirl them around in my mouth, then ask,
What is the problem?
I am your body's #1 fan.

By *your body's #1 fan* I mean you are the perfect umbrella.
Your skin is more than just water resistant.
You'll beep if I ever forget you in a shopping cart.
And strong winds will never
blow you inside out.

You ask why I had eraser shavings stuck underneath my
fingernails
when we first met. I answer,
It was a long, hard-ass problem.

By *long, hard-ass problem* I mean,
it was tough figuring out after they die,
beautiful people return as clouds.
You comb the overgrown skin from your cuticles
and lament,
It's so hard to be faithful
during a thunderstorm.

Auto Pilot

Who's to question what color looks best on you when the hue always has the final say? The most deceptive tints possess glints of emerald and wishful thinking. You notice how lovely the neighbor's front lawn is but are disappointed when you walk by and realize it's a sprayed on evergreen facade. There goes the neighborhood and welcome naysayers' creditability to the community when a lie is manicured and advertised as having front curb appeal. No pile of leaves will rake themselves up if the shovel lacks a handle and has a hole in it. If only there were cruise control for navigating how we leap from one place to another in our lives but also guides us to how those places leapt into us. Who can recall what prompted the shooter to storm into the schoolyard after recess? Who can confirm the number of bullets it takes before we begin caring about the color and consistency of kindergarteners' blood?

Growing Pains

Stretching yourself to capacity is the ultimate measure of being uncomfortable in your own skin. Allowing limbs to shape and break is like a molting that calls for a new way of life and wardrobe. New me, new Michael Kors. We're at the mercy of ourselves when stripped down to our insecurities and innards. The term *gut check* was coined after a stoic man was told to *dig deeper* by his angry wife, so he grabbed a butterknife and stuck it in his stomach. Of the approximately 500 bodies found at the Crow Creek Massacre site, 90% of the skulls show evidence of scalping. It's a myth we only use 10% of our brain. But it's a little-known fact, taking the top of men's heads as a trophy enables the fallen to feel the wind to finally flow through them as if their emotion were free to be expressed like severed apologies.

Dark Horse

A man and his stallion appeared in a small town and who pays any attention to a stranger and his steed. So when a visitor from nowhere and his horse won the local race, residents shook their heads and fists while the victors rode off with the prize money into a grinning sunset. Whenever we are not thought of to even be counted out, a new idiom is born. The surprise party originated when a man showed up to another man's 50th birthday. He walked into the living room, eager to be seen by his family after a lengthy absence, and yelled, *Surpriiiiiiiiiise!* just as the birthday boy blew out his last candle. None of the guests knew who the party-crasher was, but he helped himself and exclaimed, *I've never tasted anything as divine as the icing on the cake.* The odds of living to one hundred are 5000 to 1. The odds increase when that centenarian is a stranger in a strange land, when truth is stranger than fiction, when two birds are killed with one stone that, strangely enough, has happened twice just south of Louisville.

Center Stage

Maybe it's better the fickle wind rearranges the view. Who hasn't thought, *How fake to look at such an artificially manicured landscape?* The leaves ride the current as if mimicking the hands of a colorful conductor and the symphony is an ode to a fallen tree. Raking the lawn in A minor is synonymous with mourning the dead. We convince ourselves we have nothing left to give and call it plausible. We do the best with what we can and label it passable. To notice one's surroundings is to live as testament to Heaven. A Hells Angel pulls into the Trader Joe's parking lot and his Harley blasts a pop song about stealing sunshine. A ray is a set of straight lines passing through a single point. There is no way to deny the spotlight when we are caught blushing and red-handed.

On Learning the Lyrics to *Viva Las Vengeance* Before Attending the Panic at the Disco Concert with My 18-year-old Daughter

I learn the lyrics to the song
because concerts are more fun when singing along
rather than humming,
though one is always to be commended for performing
and composing
    a symphony of their own
    syllables.

Stuck here in the weeds
on a road that leads
to nowhere…

There are apps where you can take photos of plants
and learn all about their existence.
Pay monthly, and they can tell you if they're overwatered
or neglected,
and who doesn't wish that technology existed
during their driest seasons
so they could've just snapped a picture of their past
and known just how to nurture
the hurt?

My wife says to speak life because our words
are meant to encourage and uplift
and I give my own plants pep talks,
"Stay lean, mean,
and green."

Every moment is a replay.
I'm being buried alive.

I watch my childhood favorite baseball players die around me
and can't help but think of my parents
    who are playing in their 8th innings.

Didn't want to kill the DJ,
but it can't hurt to try.

I close my eyes and belt out the lyrics I was able to learn
to the tune of the loudest of guitar solos,
the greenest of thumbs.

Divinity

I've never been this old, hence my prostate hasn't
been this enlarged, so I haven't had this much time

to think during the drip that occurs long after first
standing at the urinal. In this instance, I think about

the Bible verse in which 42 kids were eaten by a
bear for making fun of a bald prophet and count

my blessings because I've poked my share of guys
with receding hairlines. Today my devotion said,

Sometimes God throws you a curveball, and the shocking,
grizzly scripture I ponder is a pitch I'm sure even

veteran theologians would be hard-pressed to hit.
A puzzling and destructive second nature leads to

messes that could've been cleaned up with just a
a little consideration and I've made it a habit to

always leave the seat down, even after my divorce,
as if readying myself for some form of redemption.

I wait to finish relieving the contents of my body,
a wash of waste of all I've absorbed, each drop a

testament to the cleansing of my kidneys, the
grace of patience.

Produce

I scheduled my colonoscopy and immediately thought of each word that rhymes with invasive, and how the ocean felt when the first submarine penetrated the waves must be the origin of sonar. I envision cameras swimming throughout my body in the ultimate form of self-discovery but find sorrow in that no such equipment exists to distinguish whales' laughs from their cries. If discomfort were a color, it would be the shade of a grimace, a wince, and a blowhole plugged with seaweed. My eyes will be closed throughout the process, and I'll probably be wondering if it's better to be left in the dark as you slowly drown or spend each day with a life preserver wrapped around your waist. Imagine trying to get though TSA. Knowledge is power, but where *exactly* does the strength and accountability lie in fighting a good fight versus fighting a bad one? One thing is certain, not even the most adept of doctors can guarantee the effectiveness in the ratio of apples to days.

Fine Print

Each letter is starting to look a little fuzzy,
as if hunched over and wincing from a

sucker punch to the kidney by a man who
hated their font. I strain to make out the

words on the page and why I'm not content
and wonder if *numb* is most powerful as an

action or description. The actress reveals it
has overtaken her bones but expresses when

you have cancer, the sky is bluer, so should
I be thankful I look up and mainly see gray?

I can accept the wilting, the way foliage falls
to become the beloved crunch beneath our

steps. I've learned to use context clues to
fill in what I missed and am able to confess

that has been so much. But it's the moving
on I struggle with, how not to look back at

signs that appeared so clear, even the highest
cliffs could read the footnotes before the flood.

Hazing

Large, Parachuting Spiders Could Soon Invade the East Coast, Study Finds.

I.

This is what occurs when webs
long to be woven into larger than
what they really are
and the lengths that something
so delicate will go to
just to be carried off by current
away from constraints—
   tiny parachutes spinning silk like
   the daintiest of skywriting
      as if apologizing for the subtlety
of the font.

Scientists can predict patterns of movement,
but have yet to be able to determine
the difference between fleeing and flying,
the trajectory of symmetry
        and sunrise,
but how much thought is ever given
to the strength needed to populate
a community in which the residents
feel they already know enough names
of their neighbors?

II.

My daughter is in the process of
mulling her offers and selecting her college
where she will become a Trojan, Bruin,
or Golden Bear,
and because some spiders carry their young

on their backs until they're fully developed,
I wish they could tell me how they handle
the weaving of leaving the nest
and letting go?

III.

If you've ever paused to simply admire
the veracity of clouds and thought,
I don't deserve this beauty. If I could escape
any hurt I've harvested within the earth,
I could instead live here with my head
buried forever,
perhaps it's time to forgive
yourself.

IV.

I suppose the message is this…
In a world of dark, household corners,
dare to be the rangy legs of an exploring
arachnid.
In a world of fighting mascots,
forgo any *rah-rah* and allow yourself to become
the newest member to the fraternity of
mourning fathers.

Playing Chicken

We believe our head of steam can power
enough gusto to smash through remnants of
childhood trauma and uncooperative
blood pressure.
            But the temptation of giving in to our triggers
and our craving for chili fries rivals
even the most determined of
locomotives.

I've seen men fall and sometimes land
and the beauty isn't in the recovery,
but in the way they carry their brokenness
everywhere they go,
holding their mended mess like
a pile of ash and evidence
presented before a jury of their own
plummeted peers.

I confess I've sabotaged achieving my
dreams because then
            what would I have to look forward to?

The barista tells her coworker that all her nieces
are Scorpios and I always shudder at such talk
because to reduce stars to guiding others' lives
is at best a
disservice to the sky.

Sometimes I feel survivor's guilt
when I drive by Wendy's on Christmas Eve
and see divorced dads bring burgers
to their mouths
just before closing their eyes
in prayer or plea
as if looking God in the face
seeing who will blink
first.

First Draft

I force myself to ride my bike and exercise because
my body is always tried, and initially I meant *tired,*

but I kept the typo because these days the two are
interchangeable. I maintain August is the new 50

and the season when Starbucks starts selling Pumpkin
Spice is the new middle age, but I understand just

because I only order tea doesn't mean I'm not
their target customer. A man's biological clock

is not measured in the desire to conceive but in
how he reacts each time to realizations gone by

the wayside, and I'm more botanist and philosopher
than ever and have learned to stop and smell the

roses covered in dog piss, so I ask does that make
the blooming any less beautiful? I now see details

in commercials and surmise the alpaca sticking its
long neck out from the sunroof is sorta like a

metaphor alluding to head in the clouds because
when we're rooted too much on land, we fail to

applaud the fog insulating us from ourselves. I
struggle down PCH and the Long Beach breeze

coaxes me to keep pedaling, despite the fatigue
in my legs and life, with the promise of later

bringing my green tea to my lips and guzzling
down the last few drops as if nursing a thirst that

can never really be quenched.

Blue Zones

Who's responsible for giving these places with the
highest population of centenarians such a misleading

name? Longevity doesn't necessarily equate to happiness,
so it's possible these spots christened this color match

an azure sense of life. But I'm willing to bet these
areas where a scientifically studied healthy diet and

robust sense of community and purpose reflect lives
infused with quantity AND quality, so perhaps *Golden*

Grounds or *Mellowist Yellowist Sectors* are more apt names
where each glow like a pocket of phosphorous citizens

knowing the odds of them seeing one hundred is as
great as the divide between dying young and living ten

full decades. In a recent sermon, my pastor asked the
congregation if we'd like to know everything that would

happen to us before it occurred so we could prepare
and I whispered, *Nah, man,* because who wants to spend

their life worrying about what's to come when what's
already here provides enough to test the faith of even

the most devout. Noah spent 75 years building the ark,
and Moses wandered 40 years in the desert and there's

so much to be said for surviving the famines and floods
we confused with falsehoods and mirages. I reside in a

zone the color of May and murky beach water where
the morning fog distorts my vison and the kelp cradles

my ankles as if taking census of those of us who live
on blessings and borrowed time.

Jōhatsu

In Japan it's not uncommon for a man to simply evaporate in the name of shame and new identity. He chooses to become lone resident in his own Land of Disguising Sun when he deems the consequences greater than the dishonorable sum. The Prodigal Son isn't given a name in the Bible. But maybe God bestowed upon him that alias because his birth name means absolute and unwavering, and *Thou shalt always live up to thy Christening* isn't a commandment even the most steadfast disciple could ever live up to. Though I could see how *Thou shalt not leave behind your family without a forwarding address* might've been included. Sometimes I also want to become incognito and book a one-way flight to Tokyo, but I've discovered I'm scared of heights and fear the punishing, haunting memories. Athenian prisoners in Sicily would be released if they could recite Aeschylus, and I wonder if they, too, said it was all Greek to them when they were confused. If only we could say aloud the words of our own favorite philosophers when we need to free ourselves from our own prisons to be welcomed home in the form of fancy clothes and a feast as if we'd never left.

Doodling

When the old man picking up his latte at the coffee
shop proclaimed, *It's raining but not biblical portion*

monsoons, I know drivers will still struggle navigating
these busy Long Beach streets in which tires and

intimacy aren't compatible with slowing down and
consequent traction. And when the woman next to

me tapped her foot in church throughout the service,
I wondered if it was out of habit or her personal

stenography for Pastor Ruben's words. If I had my
own pulpit, I'd tell the parishioners, *It actually ain't*

how well we're prepared for the storms, but how much water
we're able to absorb. I admit I'm more accent chair

than matchy-matchy living room set, but Noah
built the ark a hundred years before the flood,

so is a play-it-safe sectional more secure than a
blazing orange recliner that screams style AND

life preserver? We buoy through our lives seeking
our fix of caffeine or 1 Corinthians, and when the

old man brought the hot coffee cup to his face
and said, *Let me see what I have for my doodle today,*

I wanted to peer over and look, too because even
the simplest squiggles can help us stay afloat in

whatever sea we struggle to set our sails in.

Small Talk

I'd rather spend my time alone planning how to
weave my apathy into the abandoned poem about

researchers' recent discovery of carnivorous squirrels
than answering strangers' questions about weather—

easy filler for those who know how to invade
spaces but not how to defend the significance of

silence or the importance of analyzing rodents
overstuffing their cheeks with their kin's guts vs.

nuts. I overheard a women tell her friend if her
hairstyle had a name it'd be called *Depression* and

was reminded getting by in life is often a case of
survival of the wittiest. "Those who can't"

overcompensate, but "those who can" are quiet
and never caught empty-handed because they

hold their tongues, able to recognize gravity is
greater than gratuity. I left off on the stanza

where I pondered the compartmentalization of
my feelings and when the guy in front of me

turned around to mention something about
cold fronts before paying for his produce, I

screamed, *You're NOT a meteorologist!*, shocked
at my insistence. But maybe that was the

breakthrough I needed, a bridge from introversion
to introspection, a path from gatherer to hunter,

a nimbus cloud giving myself permission to
finally let it all out.

We, Too, are Judas

And he cast down the pieces of silver in the temple,
and departed, and went and hanged himself.

— Matthew 27:5

Was the betrayal in stabbing an omniscient back
or even fathoming it possible to do so, and just

how deep can a knife dig when the soul is the
epitome of eternity? If we're honest with ourselves,

we'd admit we've had our own moments where
our equivalent of 30 pieces of silver allowed

greed to supersede our beliefs. There are regrets
and there are regrets we wish could be do-overs

where we'd resurrect our personalized Edens,
but remorse sans repentance is like stalagmite

vs. stalactite—the capacity for growing up or
the act of simply falling down which makes

me ponder when someone testifies how long
they've walked with God if that includes the

detours they've taken along the way. Sometimes
when we lack the capacity to ask for forgiveness

from the ones we've hurt, we, too, find ourselves
alone in an empty field, noose threaded around

our neck, our bodies dropping to earth in a
desperate attempt to shed the weight we're

carrying, dangling body swinging like a lifeless
pendulum.

Autobiographies

My buddy often brings up his ex-wife
and mentions her name is if *vent* and *lament*
are synonyms (rather than exact rhyme)
that go together the way *course* and *divorce*
so often merge into
                                        one.
And though I've brought this to his attention,
I understand how the death of something
can live on,
                                    casting breath
          into a body bent on
             breaking.

I was thinking…
     If we all wrote novels solely of grief
and titled them after our biggest losses,
would they be a community of best sellers
or would they be relegated to dollar stores
as a reminder of the change
for the prices we paid?

The left side of my body hurts when I eat
certain foods,
so these days I select my pain
based on my pallet
and what a novel concept—
          knowing yet ignoring the hurt beforehand:
turning colorblind eye to red flags,
picking the locks of closed doors,
eating that cheesecake
          anyway!

There are days when cars keep cutting in front of you
one after the other
and other days when the sailing is smooth,
but the roads will always be tied up from
onlookers who aren't even part
                    of the wreck,
and social media speculates if it's over between
the socialite and singer after
she drops his last name on her profile,
and my buddy
whispers to himself, *It really was a good marriage.*
                                                            It really was....

Sermon

Abraham begat Isaac; and Isaac begat Jacob; and Jacob begat Judas and his brethren; And Judas begat Phares and Zara of Thamar; and Phares begat Esrom; and Esrom begat Aram;

— Matthew 1:2-3

The egg begat
the chicken and
the farmer begat
the overalls and
the middleman begat
the supermarket.

The coffee begat
the customer and
the bean begat
the roast and
the desire begat
the brand.

The strawberry begat
the pickers and
brown hands begat
ICE and
Native Americans begat
the land.

MAGA begat
the bullies and
an outdated amendment begat
the gun and
the school shooter begat
the bodies.

The Bible begat
the commandments and

scripture begat
cherry-picking and
nationalism begat
hypocrisy.

Adam begat
Eve and
the rib begat
the barbecue
and the flames begat
the fire.

Injustice begat
the boycott and
hope begat
the light and
the day begat
the struggle.

Cold Turkey

Presidential pardons extend from generals
to poultry, and quitting is easy when the

alternative is being strung from your neck
to be posthumously plucked. The body

undergoes shock when deprived of debauchery,
and withdrawal often means vomiting up your

esophagus making *gutting it out* the Poorman's
rehab; I've learned gluten and glutton have

more in common than one might think, and
weaning off begins with convicting oneself

to a sentence of gallows or grace. Before
tales of a November feast, the Pilgrims

locked offenders in the pillory to enforce
religious conformity, hands and head

bound by Birch and a sense of belonging,
so how can their Northeast hospitality be

confused with exterminating Indigenous
dinner guests? The key to any dinner party

is remembering just desserts are best served
with friendliness and force-fed. The key to

developing empathy is recalling the gobble
before the last breath.

Hypothermia

Survivalists compete to see who can live isolated in the wilderness the longest carrying only a backpack and a Slinky. The winner gets a million dollars. The losers come home with a new appreciation for Mother Nature and appear on morning shows promoting cookbooks with recipes for sautéed crickets. The loudest insects are richest in protein and lipids. Isn't life most often a case of man vs. self, man vs. nature, or man vs. the amount of salmonella the body can withstand while continuing to build a makeshift log cabin? Many have mistaken a gut check for endurance but failed to see that being alone with your thoughts and bowels is the ultimate in intimacy. All the contestants have to do is push a button and a camera crew will sail out to the dwelling they've made and return them to the security of their lives. But who doesn't want to see how far they can push themselves in the name of personal challenge and reality TV? I observe all of this while spending the day binging the series in my bedroom. And as I finish the last episode, I feel so cold. So hungry. So alone.

Riding the Subway with My Son

August 8, 2024

He said it took a year to learn the routes
and he often got lost because he
fell asleep and woke up far from
    his stop.

You don't need to be a resident to
know how life can speed by before realizing
you were supposed to exit,
but it helps to understand Uptown and
Downtown run opposite directions and
    chess in Central Park is as strategic as
    window-shopping along the streets of
        SoHo.

How one knows where they're supposed to be means
learning when to remain seated and when to
    get up and pay your way or
    jump through the turnstiles,
even if you don't yet know your way around
the boroughs or your
burgeoning self.

I'm a first-time passenger and sit beside my son,
a twentysomething Brooklyn resident fluent in
traversing the lines,
and we ride through tunnels
that stretch below the earth—
a hazy maze of metal and movement,
not unlike the lifetime relationship between
a parent and child,
and I navigate just how far
we've come,
the distance we have yet to
go.

Found Poem from a Letter Written to My Daughter on her Gradation Day Combined with an End-of-Year Note I Wrote to a Parent of One of My Underachieving Students

When you first began high school
I suggested home studies.

I've had numerous talks with
the many sides of yourself
and she allows her boredom to supersede
performance.

She can be on track,
but excelling in academics and absences
isn't an achievement.

Yet I love that you took chances.
I was always too scared to pray…
proceed... prosper.

You had the right mindset at such a young age.
The loss I feel is simply
where she went wrong.

You made memories
at your own progress and pace and
I'm excited for all that awaits.

As this season comes to an end,
my suggestion for next year is
allow yourself to embrace the many sides
of both sadness and pride.

Love,
Mr. Romo/
Dad

Spirit

Who among us can calculate the hypotenuse
of Heaven?

Which sinner down below can decipher
      the formula for salvation and
an unknown variable?

Being swallowed and then stranded in the belly of a whale
is every dark place you were in
before managing to find and light the wick coded in better days
                                        and belief.

No one beats around a burning bush when concerning
the volume of eternity.

What happens when the body exposes the destination of the soul?

There's no question too complex to be answered in time
                and transcendence.

Deductibles

The driver's side of my car was introduced
to a woman running late for her job
as a security officer.
And I hope she's better at looking out for
bad guys than looking out for
cars in the right lane already occupied by guys
simply wanting to get home to take a nap
          after work.

There are first impressions that leave no impact
and there are first impressions that result in
whiplash and trips
                    to urgent care,
where I took X-rays and tilted my shoulder in
various positions to capture its most flattering
and damaged angle and wondered
which photo would ultimately be selected
                              for the yearbook.

But I hurt more for the husband who walked
alongside his wife battling dementia,
whom we know was afflicted because he
informed all the other patients as his wife
stroked the hair of the little girl she didn't know
and looked through each our faces as if
recalling all the places
          we never met.
Gloria wakes up in the same position I lay her down,
he tells any of us who will understand
how it feels to be blindsided by a Chrysler
or illness
          you never saw coming.

Sometimes even staying in your own lane
obeying the speed limit gives no opportunity
to swerve out of the way,
and even the brightest headlights can't warn you
of accidents that lie ahead.

I took my car to the garage to get an estimate,
thankful it could be repaired,
aware that there are instances
no insurance can ever really
cover.

Cheeeese

I cut off my nose to spite my face and I've never smelled more clearly. I make extra-long stops to smell the roses, fresh bread, and even trouble, as if inhaling and savoring virgin scents enhanced by this extraordinary gaping hole in my head. But my eyes and ears aren't sure what to make of my newly found sensation and also beg to be severed. My vision is failing in protest as if preparing for a strike where the line is drawn in the skin with a sharp knife. Sounds are becoming muddled as if each syllable is giving an inaudible ultimatum. I decide such is life and not to let the envy dictate my mood but notice my smile becoming heavier to uphold. Even body parts aren't immune to the effects of the seven deadly sins. I bring the blade to my stoic face, knowing what must be done.

Sunday League

For Jason

As men age, we wear gray in our beards like
an errant fastball to the ribs
that escaped the pitcher's hand
because we've learned not to rub it
and acknowledge the pain
no matter how hard the hurt
we absorb.

I've had my share of traumatic, postgame at-bats
and the satisfaction in getting on base from a hit
vs. four wayward pitches
is sweeter because earning your way
is always greater than being
rewarded for another man's
failure.

We play games of some sort all our lives
because guys like us have DNA composed of
adrenaline and competitiveness,
and I'll bet even though my knees
may disagree,
I can still run down any fly ball
and get down for any grounder
I failed to field in my past.

Jason...
your name means *healer,*
and I still recall the way you used to
walk to the mound from behind the plate
to tell your pitcher to simply relax
as if your reassuring words
cured the flatness of his curve,
the unsteadiness of his nerves.

There will come a day when we, too,
play our last game in this life—
rounding third,
deciding if we should take our chances
and stand up,
or if we need to slide
and pray
our way
            into home.

Last Will

While hurrying home from work to read my favorite
poet's last book, put together by his wife after the

cancer he so beautifully captured ensured his words
would never touch anyone again, I see a man selling

shoes in the parking lot of a sketchy strip mall
and wonder if his goods for sale are like the taco

vendors'—so delicious the city overlooks the need
for a permit due to his contribution to a hungry

community. I question how much money he can
possibly make since I'm sure most motorists won't

stop because stolen Jordans don't wet the appetite
like grilled carne asada. I thought I'd have a

different teaching job by now, but I still chide
and lecture teens and the numerous interviews

I've been a part of haven't proven lucrative enough
to sell to a panel of college professors who scrutinize

my words and wear comfortable Rockports. I hope
Tony made it to Heaven and before he stood in

front of God, surrendered his soul and unflattering
similes, and God accepted him and didn't pass him

over for another candidate simply due to perceived
lack of experience. When my wife does the laundry

and tells me I keep leaving candy wrappers in my
pants pockets, I don't tell her that maybe they're

in there purposely because I want her to always
remember me because she was able to unwrap

the man that I am, and that is the best poetry
I can ever leave behind for her.

On 8th and Pine

The fight is up for grabs when
neither man can throw a punch
because a gust of wild haymakers
is akin to a multitude of prayers
from those who've never bowed
their heads but just learned they're
dying of a disease difficult to
pronounce, while the skater
connects on a combination of tricks
and you can tell he's devoted to a
life of shuv-its and kickflips and
grinds between the bottom of his
board and benches create a holy
union after a series of impromptu
consummations. I'm most me when
my surroundings resemble all that
I'm not: the chihuahua pissing in
a planter and prancing off, the
delivery truck bringing its immense
weight to a stop in front of a taqueria
that reeks of long hours and grease.
Because what we have here is slice
of life divided into segments so clear,
you realize how you end the poem is
how you begin the rest
of your life.

About the Author

Daniel Romo is the author of *American Manscape* (Moon Tide Press 2026), *Bum Knees and Grieving Sunsets* (Flower Song Press 2023), *Moonlighting as an Avalanche* (Tebot Bach 2021), and other books. He received an MFA from Queens University of Charlotte, and he teaches high school English. More at danieljromo.com.

Acknowledgements

Always Crashing: “From 1915 Rules for Teacher Found Poem”

The Bookends Review: “Election”

Clayjar Review: “Green Thumb”

Cobra Milk: 2nd: “Hypothermia,” “Street Baptismal”

Copihue Poetry: “Dad Jokes,” “Playing Chicken,”
“Season Passholder”

Eastern Iowa Review: “June Gloom”

First Literary Review-East: “Growing Pains”

Gone Lawn: “Auto Pilot”

Hamilton Stone Review: “Imposter Syndrome”

Hear of Flesh: “Spirit,” “We, Too, are Judas”

Like a Field: “Forecast”

The Literary Underground: “Empty Nest,” “Pamplona,”
“Small Talk”

The Meadowlark Review: “On Learning the Lyrics to
Viva Las Vengeance Before Attending the Panic at the Disco
Concert with my 18-year-old Daughter”

Mixtape Review: “On 8th and Pine”

New Verse News: “Blading,” “Diss Track,” “Sermon”

One Art: “Second Marriage”

OxMag: "Sunday League"

¡Pa'lante!: "Taking Roll"

Peatsmoke: "Happy Hour"

Pensive: "Proclamation"

Poor Yorick: "Playing R&B On My Way to Work While Driving Down PCH"

Reverie: "House Specials"

Rigorous: "Blowing Out Candles," "Deductibles," "Found Poem from a Letter Written to My Daughter on her Gradation Day Combined with an End-of-Year Note I Wrote to a Parent of One of My Underachieving Students," "Hazing"

San Antonio Review: "Blue Zone," "Last Night Just Before Midnight I Ordered Calvin Klein Boxer Briefs on eBay," "Last Will"

The Skinny Poetry Journal: "New Reign"

Somos en Escrito: "Center Stage"

South Carolina Review: "Acupressure" "Produce"

Spotlong Review: "Maritime"

Sublunary Review: "Spam"

Temporal Lobe Literary: "Half Day"

Thrush: "Variables"

Trampoline: "Forget-me-nots"

UCity Review: "Autobiographies"

Underscore Magazine: "Doodling"

White Wall Review: "Passengers"

Winged Penny Review: "Lines that Stuck Out After Watching *The Notebook* for the First Time at 49 or Things I say to Myself 6 Months from When I Turn 50?"

Wrong Turn Lit: "August," "First Draft"

Also Available from Moon Tide Press

Frozen Fawn, Ally McGregor (2026)
The Ground Never Lets Go, Liz Marlow (2026)
Afterburn, Rebecca Evans (2026)
Not So Fast, Sarah McMahon (2026)
The Elephant of Surprise, Charles Harper Webb (2026)
Outliving Michael, Steven Reigns (2025)
Prayers With a Side of Cash, Kathleen Florence (2025)
Somewhere, a Playground, Rich Ferguson (2025)
The Tautology of Water, Giovanni Boskovich (2025)
Take Care, Mark Danowsky (2025)
Dilapitatia, Kelly Gray (2025)
Reluctant Prophets, J.D. Isip (2025)
Enormous Blue Umbrella, Donna Hilbert (2025)
Sky Leaning Toward Winter, Terri Niccum (2024)
Living the Sundown: A Caregiving Memoir,
G. Murray Thomas (2024)
Figure Study, Kathryn de Lancellotti (2024)
Suffer for This: Love, Sex, Marriage, & Rock 'N' Roll,
Victor D. Infante (2024)
What Blooms in the Dark, Emily J. Mundy (2024)
Fable, Bryn Wickerd (2024)
Diamond Bars 2, David A. Romero (2024)
Safe Handling, Rebecca Evans (2024)
More Jerkumstances: New & Selected Poems,
Barbara Eknoian (2024)
Dissection Day, Ally McGregor (2023)
He's a Color Until He's Not, Christian Hanz Lozada (2023)
The Language of Fractions, Nicelle Davis (2023)
Paradise Anonymous, Oriana Ivy (2023)
Now You Are a Missing Person, Susan Hayden (2023)
Maze Mouth, Brian Sonia-Wallace (2023)
Tangled by Blood, Rebecca Evans (2023)
Another Way of Loving Death, Jeremy Ra (2023)
Kissing the Wound, J.D. Isip (2023)
Feed It to the River, Terhi K. Cherry (2022)

Beat Not Beat: An Anthology of California Poets Screwing on the Beat and Post-Beat Tradition (2022)
When There Are Nine: Poems Celebrating the Life and Achievements of Ruth Bader Ginsburg (2022)
The Knife Thrower's Daughter, Terri Niccum (2022)
2 Revere Place, Aruni Wijesinghe (2022)
Here Go the Knives, Kelsey Bryan-Zwick (2022)
Trumpets in the Sky, Jerry Garcia (2022)
Threnody, Donna Hilbert (2022)
A Burning Lake of Paper Suns, Ellen Webre (2021)
Instructions for an Animal Body, Kelly Gray (2021)
*Head *V* Heart: New & Selected Poems*, Rob Sturma (2021)
Sh!t Men Say to Me: A Poetry Anthology in Response to Toxic Masculinity (2021)
Flower Grand First, Gustavo Hernandez (2021)
Everything is Radiant Between the Hates, Rich Ferguson (2020)
When the Pain Starts: Poetry as Sequential Art, Alan Passman (2020)
This Place Could Be Haunted If I Didn't Believe in Love, Lincoln McElwee (2020)
Impossible Thirst, Kathryn de Lancellotti (2020)
Lullabies for End Times, Jennifer Bradpiece (2020)
Crabgrass World, Robin Axworthy (2020)
Contortionist Tongue, Dania Ayah Alkhouli (2020)
The only thing that makes sense is to grow, Scott Ferry (2020)
Dead Letter Box, Terri Niccum (2019)
Tea and Subtitles: Selected Poems 1999-2019, Michael Miller (2019)
At the Table of the Unknown, Alexandra Umlas (2019)
The Book of Rabbits, Vince Trimboli (2019)
Everything I Write Is a Love Song to the World, David McIntire (2019)
Letters to the Leader, HanaLena Fennel (2019)
Darwin's Garden, Lee Rossi (2019)
Dark Ink: A Poetry Anthology Inspired by Horror (2018)
Drop and Dazzle, Peggy Dobreer (2018)
Junkie Wife, Alexis Rhone Fancher (2018)
The Moon, My Lover, My Mother, & the Dog, Daniel McGinn (2018)

Lullaby of Teeth: An Anthology of Southern California Poetry (2017)
Angels in Seven, Michael Miller (2016)
A Likely Story, Robbi Nester (2014)
Embers on the Stairs, Ruth Bavetta (2014)
The Green of Sunset, John Brantingham (2013)
The Savagery of Bone, Timothy Matthew Perez (2013)
The Silence of Doorways, Sharon Venezio (2013)
Cosmos: An Anthology of Southern California Poetry (2012)
Straws and Shadows, Irena Praitis (2012)
In the Lake of Your Bones, Peggy Dobreer (2012)
I Was Building Up to Something, Susan Davis (2011)
Hopeless Cases, Michael Kramer (2011)
One World, Gail Newman (2011)
What We Ache For, Eric Morago (2010)
Now and Then, Lee Mallory (2009)
Pop Art: An Anthology of Southern California Poetry (2009)
In the Heaven of Never Before, Carine Topal (2008)
A Wild Region, Kate Buckley (2008)
Carving in Bone: An Anthology of Orange County Poetry (2007)
Kindness from a Dark God, Ben Trigg (2007)
A Thin Strand of Lights, Ricki Mandeville (2006)
Sleepyhead Assassins, Mindy Nettifee (2006)
Tide Pools: An Anthology of Orange County Poetry (2006)
Lost American Nights: Lyrics & Poems, Michael Ubaldini (2006)

Patrons

Moon Tide Press would like to thank the following people for their support in helping publish the finest poetry from the Southern California region. To sign up as a patron, visit www.moontidepress.com or send an email to publisher@moontidepress.com.

Anonymous
Robin Axworthy
Conner Brenner
Nicole Connolly
Bill Cushing
Susan Davis
Kristen Baum DeBeasi
Peggy Dobreer
Kate Gale
Dennis Gowans
Alexis Rhone Fancher
HanaLena Fennel
Half Off Books & Brad T. Cox
Donna Hilbert
Jim & Vicky Hoggatt
Michael Kramer
Ron Koertge & Bianca Richards
Gary Jacobelly
Ray & Christi Lacoste
Jeffery Lewis
Zachary & Tammy Locklin
Lincoln McElwee
David McIntire
José Enrique Medina
Michael Miller &
Rachanee Srisavasdi
Michelle & Robert Miller
Ronny & Richard Morago
Terri Niccum
Andrew November
Jeremy Ra
Luke & Mia Salazar
Jennifer Smith
Roger Sponder
Andrew Turner
Rex Wilder
Mariano Zaro
Wes Bryan Zwick

www.ingramcontent.com/pod-product-compliance
Lightning Source LLC
LaVergne TN
LVHW051014080826
845145LV00009B/2610

* 9 7 8 1 9 5 7 7 9 9 5 4 4 *